A Note to Parents and Teachers

Kids can imagine, kids can laugh and kids can learn to read
with this exciting new series of first readers. Each book in the
Kids Can Read series has been especially written, illustrated and
designed for beginning readers. Humorous, easy-to-read stories,
appealing characters and topics, and engaging illustrations make
for books that kids will want to read over and over again.

To make selecting a book easy for kids, parents and teachers,
the Kids Can Read series offers three levels based on different
reading abilities:

Level 1: Kids Can Start to Read

Short stories, simple sentences, easy vocabulary, lots of repetition
and visual clues for kids just beginning to read.

Level 2: Kids Can Read with Help

Longer stories, varied sentences, increased vocabulary, some
repetition and visual clues for kids who have some reading skills,
but may need a little help.

Level 3: Kids Can Read Alone

More challenging topics, more complex sentences, advanced
vocabulary, language play, minimal repetition and visual clues
for kids who are reading by themselves.

With the Kids Can Read series, kids can enter a new and exciting
world of reading!

How Animals Move

Written by Pamela Hickman
Illustrated by Pat Stephens

Kids Can Press

To Caitlin — P.S.

⭐ **Kids Can Read** ® Kids Can Read is a registered trademark of Kids Can Press Ltd.

Text © 2000 Pamela Hickman
Illustrations © 2000 Pat Stephens
Revised edition © 2007

Kids Can Press acknowledges the financial support of the Government of Ontario, through the Ontario Media Development Corporation's Ontario Book Initiative; the Ontario Arts Council; the Canada Council for the Arts; and the Government of Canada, through the BPIDP, for our publishing activity.

Published in Canada by
Kids Can Press Ltd.
29 Birch Avenue
Toronto, ON M4V 1E2

Published in the U.S. by
Kids Can Press Ltd.
2250 Military Road
Tonawanda, NY 14150

www.kidscanpress.com

Adapted by David MacDonald from the book *Animals in Motion*.

Edited by David MacDonald
Designed by Sherill Chapman
Educational consultant: Maureen Skinner Weiner, United Synagogue Day School, Willowdale, Ontario

Printed and bound in Singapore

The hardcover edition of this book is smyth sewn casebound.
The paperback edition of this book is limp sewn with a drawn-on cover.

CM 07 0 9 8 7 6 5 4 3 2 1
CM PA 07 0 9 8 7 6 5 4 3 2 1

Library and Archives Canada Cataloguing in Publication

Hickman, Pamela
   How animals move / written by Pamela Hickman ; illustrated by Pat Stephens.

(Kids Can read)
Based on author's Animals in motion.

ISBN-13: 978-1-55453-029-8 (bound) ISBN-10: 1-55453-029-6 (bound)
ISBN-13: 978-1-55453-030-4 (pbk.) ISBN-10: 1-55453-030-X (pbk.)

1. Animal locomotion — Juvenile literature. I. Stephens, Pat, 1950– II. Title.
III. Series: Kids Can read (Toronto, Ont.)

QP301.H52 2007   j573.7'9   C2006-903043-X

Kids Can Press is a ℓ⊙ℝUS™ Entertainment company

Contents

On the move

What would it be like to run faster than a car?
A cheetah knows. What if you could jump a
tall fence in one leap? A kangaroo can.

Animals have different bodies that help them
move in different ways. Get ready to meet
some interesting animals on the move!

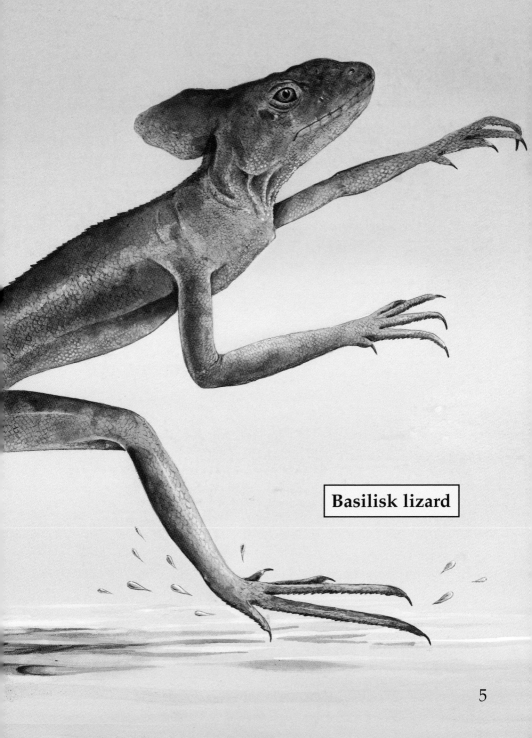

Basilisk lizard

Swimmers and floaters

Animals that live in water have special bodies that help them swim or float. Being a good swimmer or diver helps these animals catch food and get away from enemies.

Beavers are very good at both swimming and diving.

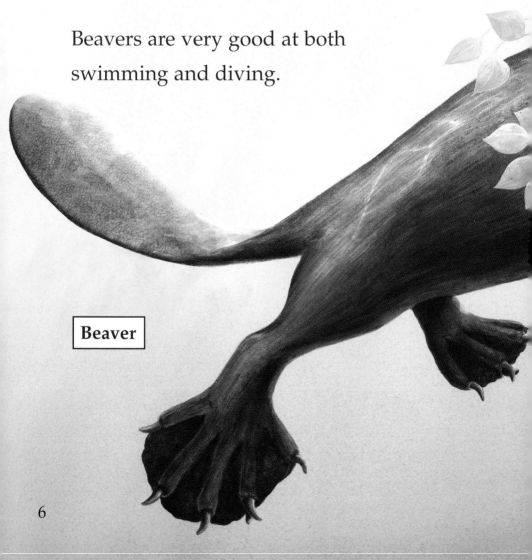

Beaver

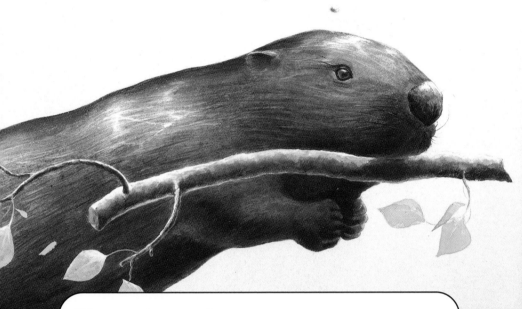

If you were a beaver ...

- you would have flaps of skin between the toes on your back feet. These flaps would help you swim.

- your wide, flat tail would help you steer through the water.

- you could close tiny flaps in your nose and ears so water couldn't get in.

Go fish

A fish uses its fins to help it move through the water. Pectoral fins help the fish turn. The tail fin helps push the fish through the water, and it also helps the fish steer.

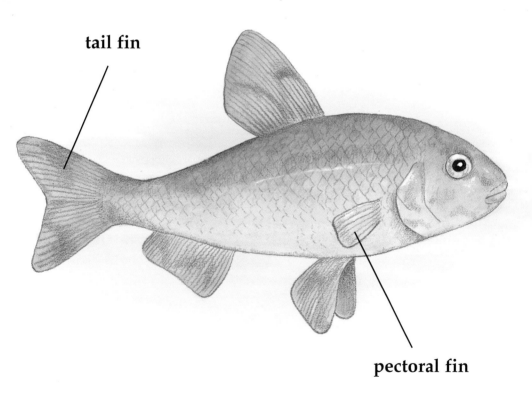

tail fin

pectoral fin

Wings underwater

The manta ray's body is
flat and thin, like a pancake.
This body shape lets it move
easily through the water.

Manta ray

On each side of its body, the manta ray has
two large fins that look like wings. These
fins help it swim. The long, thin tail helps
with steering.

A penguin's narrow, pointy wings make great underwater flippers that help with swimming and diving.

Penguin

Puffins use their short wings for flying in the air and for swimming underwater.

Puffin

Webbed feet

Many animals that swim have built-in flippers called webbed feet. You can see the beaver's webbed feet on page 6, and the webbed feet of the otter on page 27.

Frogs are famous for their large webbed feet. The duck-billed platypus also has webbed feet to help it swim.

Duck-billed platypus

Fliers and gliders

Many animals can move through the air, but it takes wings to really fly. A honeybee can flap its wings 250 times in one second. A hummingbird can do 75 flaps in a second.

All that flapping takes a lot of energy. That's why honeybees and hummingbirds spend most of their time feeding.

Hummingbird

If you were a hummingbird ...

- you could fly forward, backward, up, down, sideways and upside down.
- you could flap your wings and stay in one place to feed on a flower.
- your wings would flap so quickly that they would make a humming sound.

Winging it

Bats don't have feathers.
Their wings are made
of a thin layer of skin
that stretches
over long
finger bones.

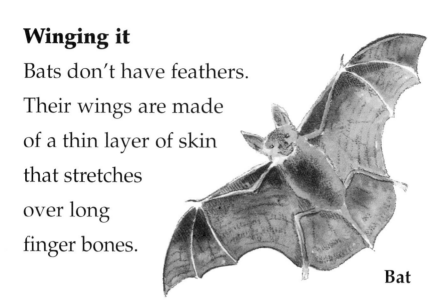

Bat

Insects such as dragonflies have four wings.
When the front wings move up, the back
wings move down. Bees, moths and
butterflies also have four wings. Their
front and back
wings move
up and down
at the same time.

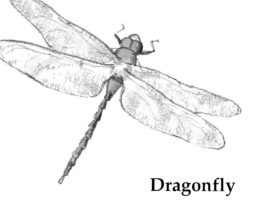

Dragonfly

Gliding through the air

People use parachutes to make them fall more slowly through the air. Many animals have built-in parachutes.

When a flying squirrel wants to move from tree to tree, it jumps into the air. Then it spreads its legs out wide. The flaps of skin between its front and back legs act like parachutes. They let the squirrel glide through the air.

Flying squirrel

Runners and walkers

When you walk, the bottom of your whole foot touches the ground. But if you were a bird, a cat or a dog, you would walk only on your toes.

The cheetah is a fantastic runner. It must run very quickly to catch the animals it wants to eat.

Cheetah

If you were a cheetah …

- you could run faster than any other animal on Earth.

- you would have extra-long legs and strong muscles in your back legs.

- your long claws would help you grip the ground as you run.

Fancy feet

Some animals have special feet that make it easier to get around.

The desert camel has wide, flat pads on the bottoms of its feet. The pads make it easier to walk across sand without sinking.

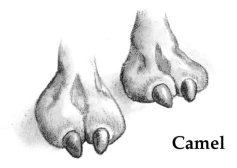

Camel

In winter, the ruffed grouse grows a special set of scales along its toes. The scales keep it from sinking into the snow.

Ruffed grouse

Walking on water

Have you ever seen a bird walk on water? Jacanas can walk across floating plants by spreading out their long toes.

Jacana

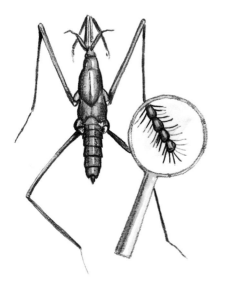

Water strider

If you use a magnifying glass to look at the feet of a water strider, you'll see why it can walk on water. The tiny hairs on its feet help keep it from sinking.

Hoppers and jumpers

If you had to jump everywhere instead of walk, you'd soon get tired. But if you were a flea, you could jump more than 10 000 times in an hour and still have energy left over. Many animals hop and jump to move quickly and escape enemies. That's what the kangaroo rat does.

If you were a kangaroo rat …

- you would have long, strong back legs for jumping.
- your long tail would help you balance and turn quickly in midair.
- you would have large, hairy back feet to keep you from sinking in sand.
- you would jump in a zigzag pattern to escape from enemies.

Kangaroo rat

Jumpy critters

If you could jump as well as a grasshopper can, you would be able to travel the length of a football field in just three jumps!

How can insects such as grasshoppers, leafhoppers and fleas jump such a long way? They have strong leg muscles and small bodies that don't weigh very much.

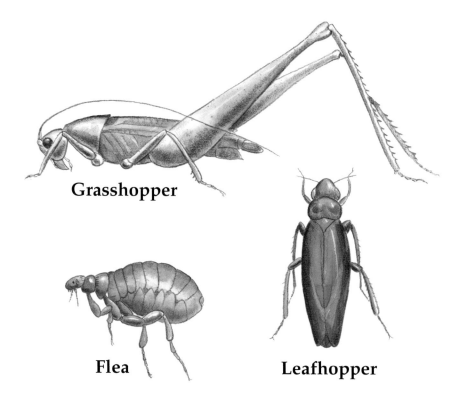

Grasshopper

Flea

Leafhopper

High jumpers

Which animal do you think can jump the highest — a kangaroo or a snowshoe hare? Believe it or not, a snowshoe hare can jump nearly twice as high as a kangaroo.

Big, strong back legs and large feet make both these animals great jumpers.

Snowshoe hare

Kangaroo

Slippers and sliders

Snakes and other animals without legs are experts at sliding. Some can even slide up trees to look for food or to escape danger.

Some creatures, such as earthworms, slugs and snails, like to come out in the rain because the wet ground is easier to slide on.

Snail

If you were a snail ...

- you would have only one foot.
- your body would make a slimy goo that makes it easier for you to slide across the ground.
- you would move very slowly — less than 3 cm (1 in.) in a minute.

Slithering snakes

Different kinds of snakes move in different ways.

The boa constrictor moves in a straight line, like a caterpillar. It moves the front of its body forward and then pulls the rest of its body along to "catch up."

Boa constrictor

The garter snake pushes against stones and other objects to move its body in an S-shape over the ground.

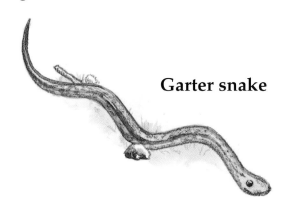

Garter snake

Cool moves

Otters like to slide! Otter families often slide on their bellies along a frozen trail that goes down to a lake or river. In summer, otters slide down mud trails and land in the water below.

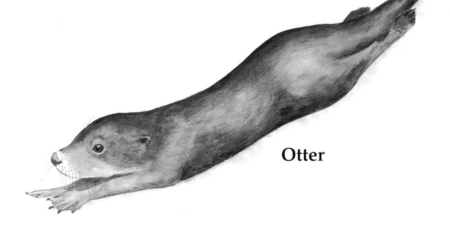

Otter

When otters slide, they stretch out their front legs. Their back legs stick out beside their tail.

Climbers and swingers

Many kinds of animals spend their lives in trees — eating, sleeping and moving through the treetops. Animals that feed on the ground may sleep in trees to stay safe from enemies.

Some animals have bodies that help them swing through trees or hold on to branches.

Tree frog

28

If you were a tree frog ...

- your toes would end in sticky round pads, like suction cups, to help you hang on as you climb.
- your toes could turn sideways and backward so you could climb without having to let go.

Fingers, toes and tails

The spider monkey has extra-long arms and long fingers and toes. These make it easy to reach out and grab branches while swinging through trees.

Spider monkey

A spider monkey can use its long tail like an extra arm for holding on.

Spider monkeys and gibbons have special hands that are bent into a hook shape to make it easier to grab the next branch.

A gibbon can move very quickly as it swings through trees.

Gibbon

Slow down

The three-toed sloth moves from place to place while it hangs upside down from tree branches. It holds on with its huge, curved claws.

The sloth creeps along a tree branch very, very slowly. It is the slowest mammal on Earth!

Three-toed sloth